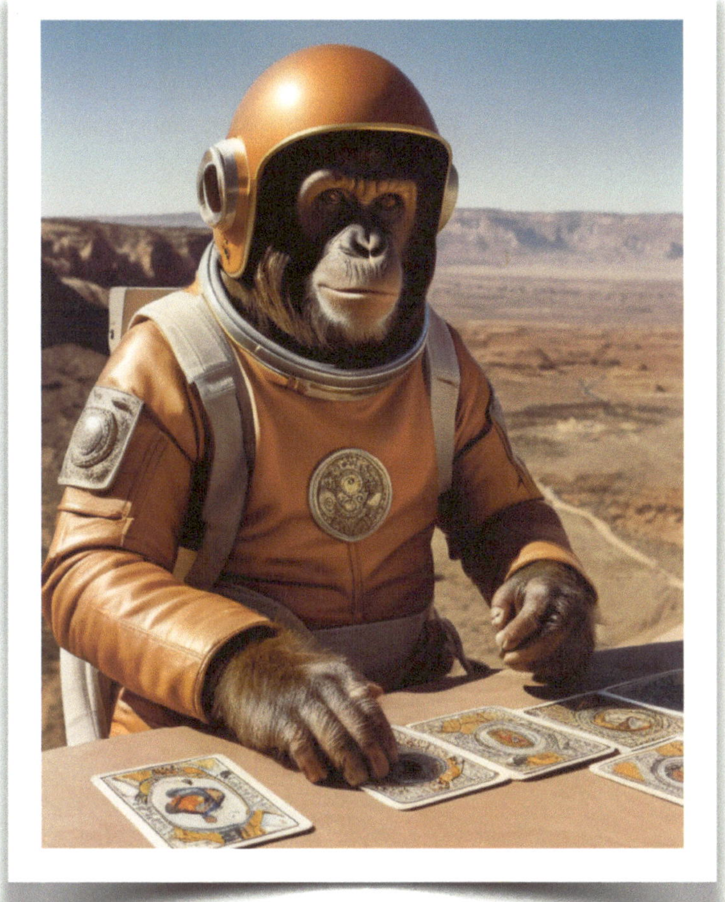

1

PLANET OF THE TAROTS

i TAROCCHI delle SCIMMIE

by Simone Gallina

INTRO

This new volume is part of a collection of conceptual tarot cards.

The theme is that of the 22 characters of the Major Arcana Tarot cards brought into the world of The Planet of The Apes.

Each card has been freely interpreted, inspired by the fabulous world of primates.

I thought I would test my creativity at matching description given to an AI engine, so that they would capture the varied forms of this species.

I am therefore adding this tarot series to the collection of my previous ones, hoping it will intrigue.

The Author

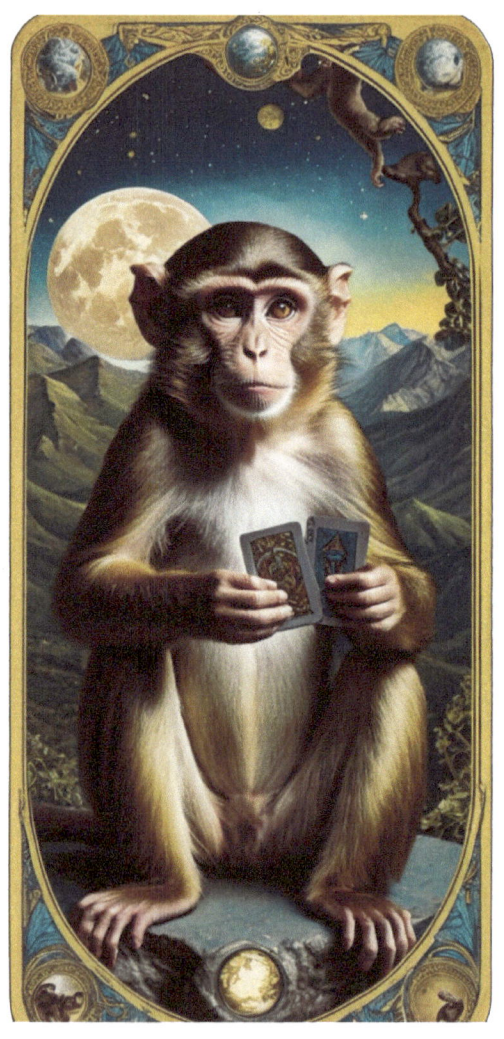

6

INDEX

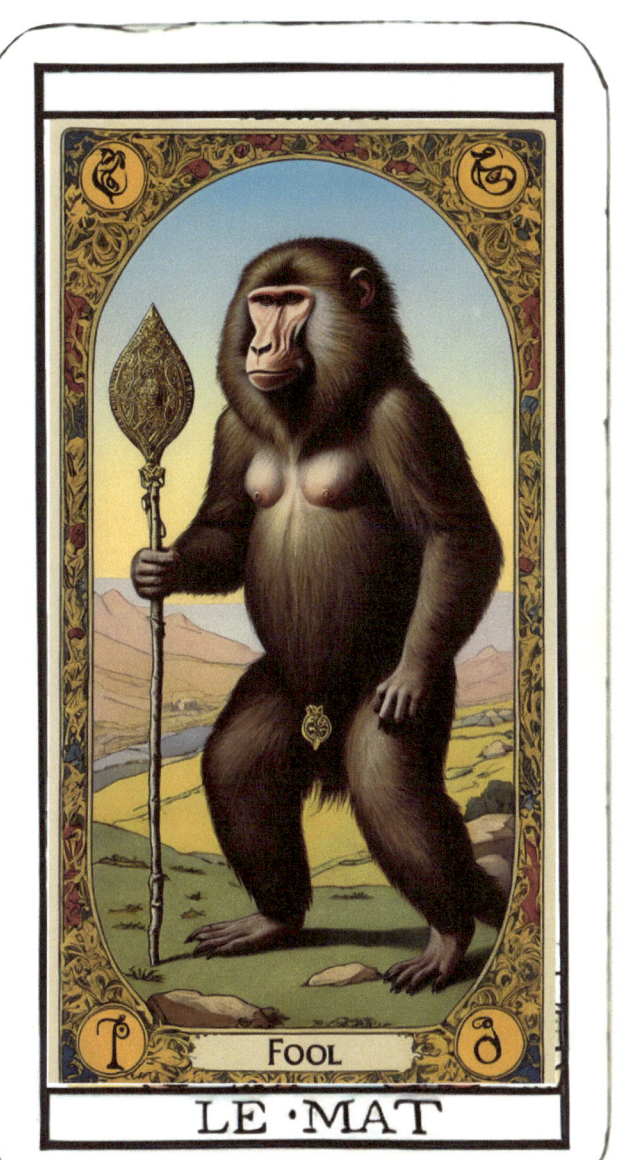

FOOL

LE ·MAT

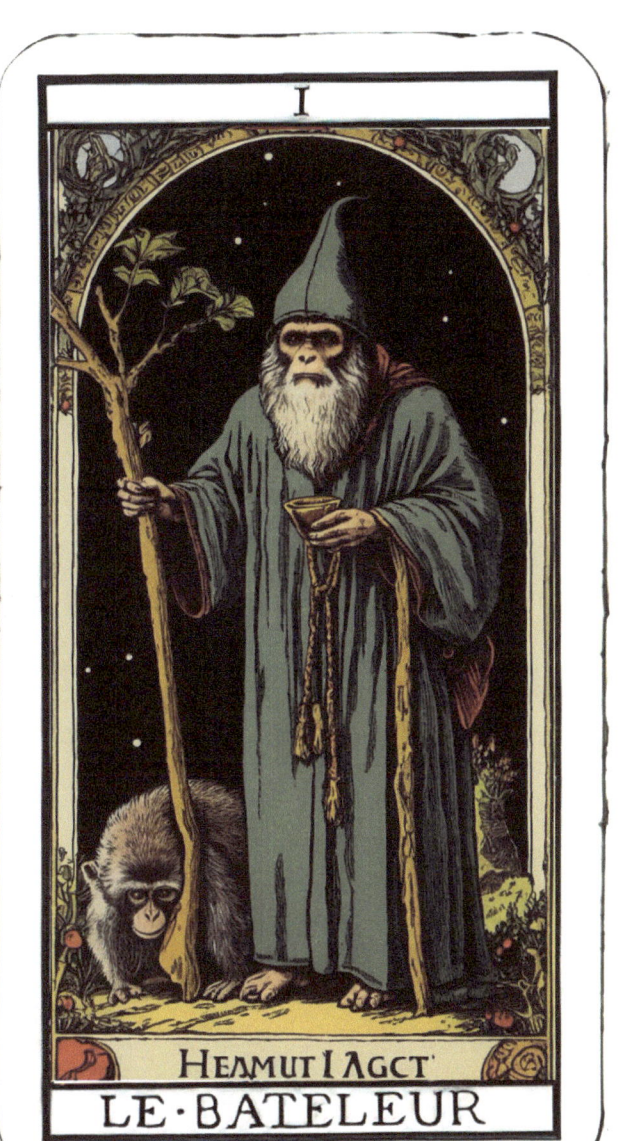

I

HEAMUT I AGCT

LE·BATELEUR

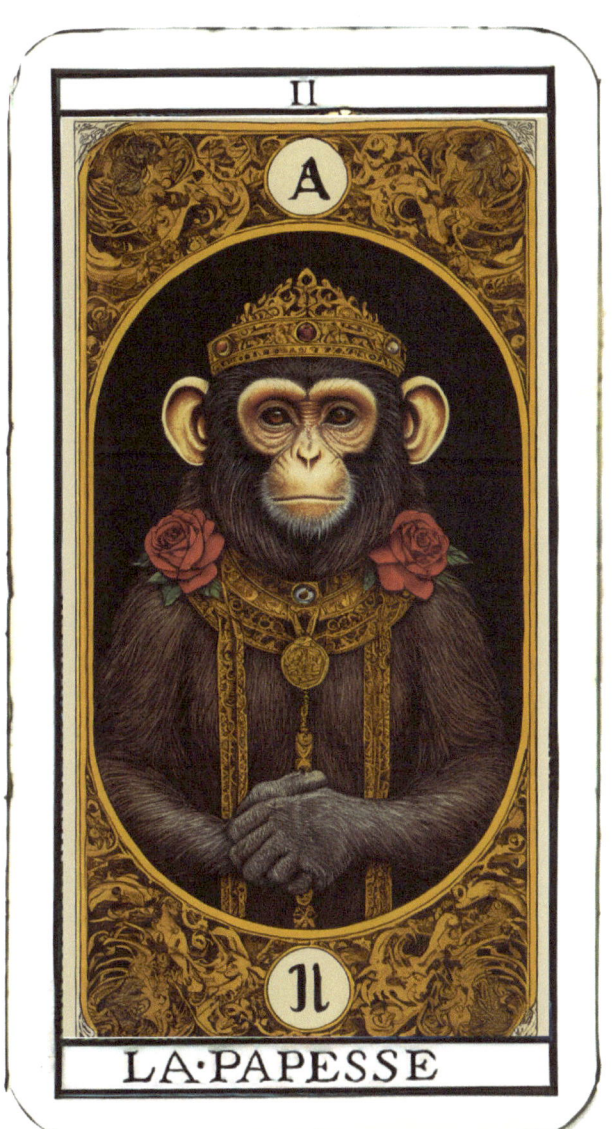

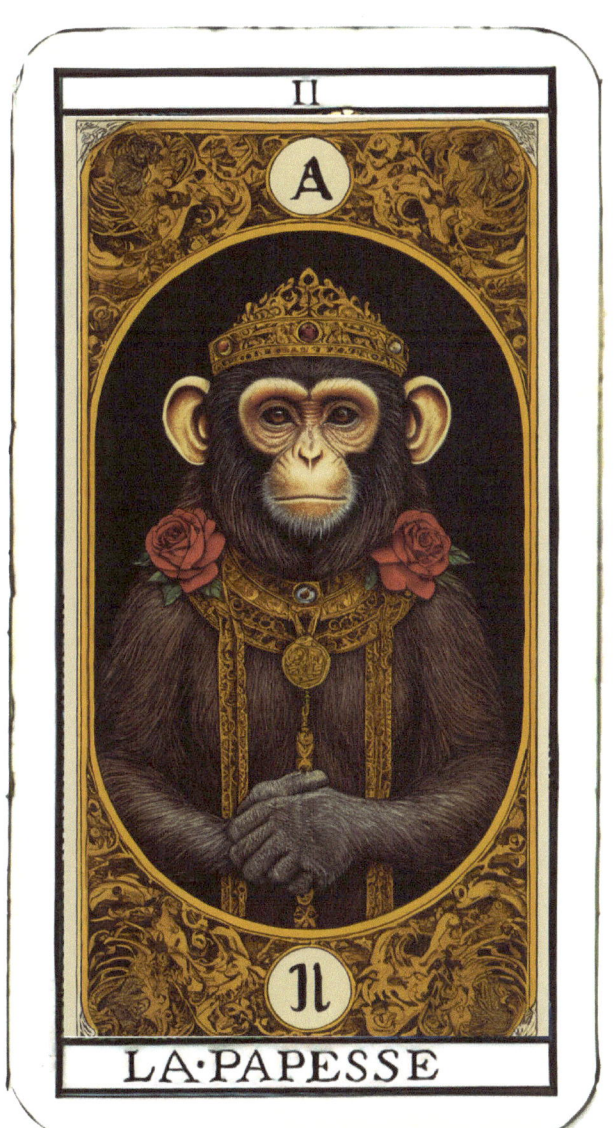

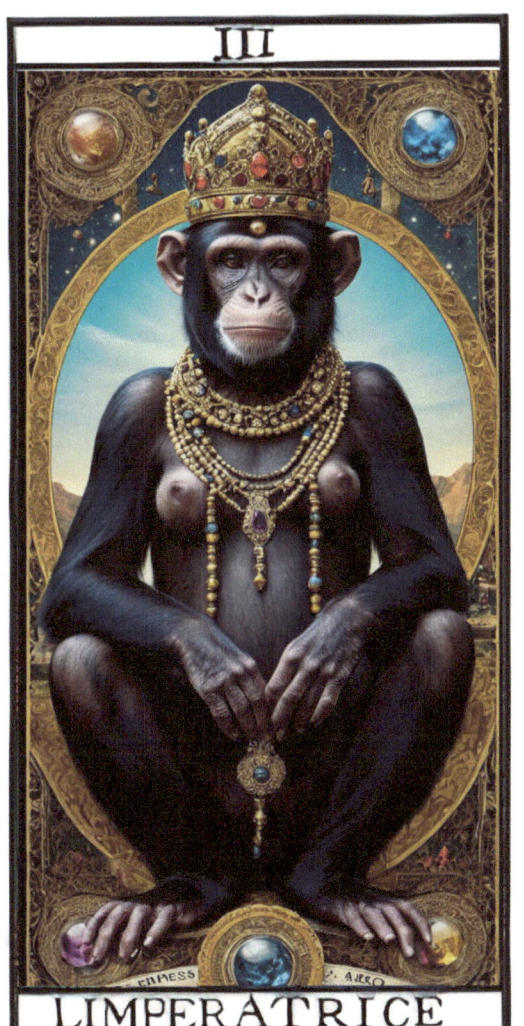

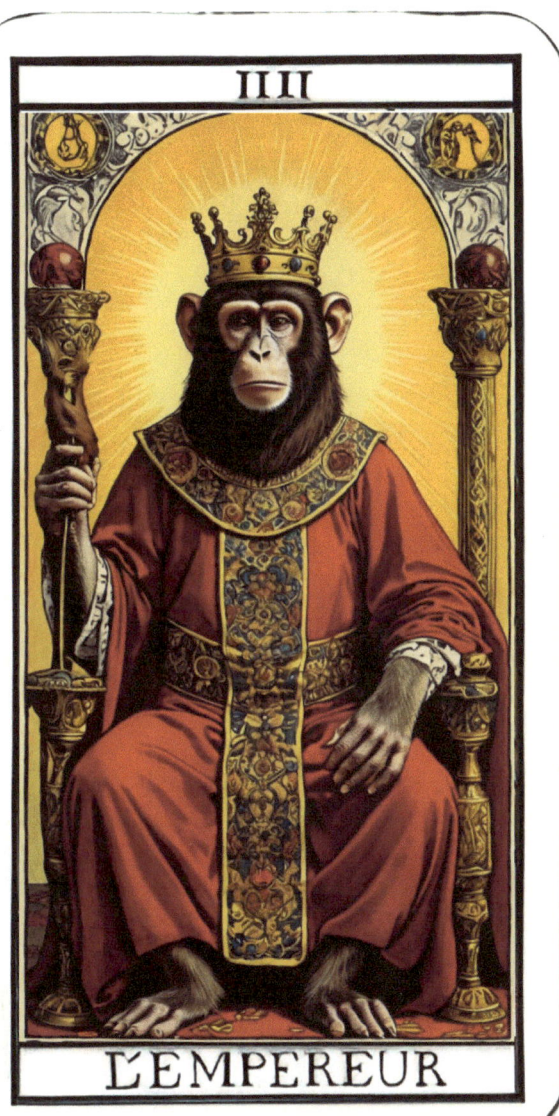

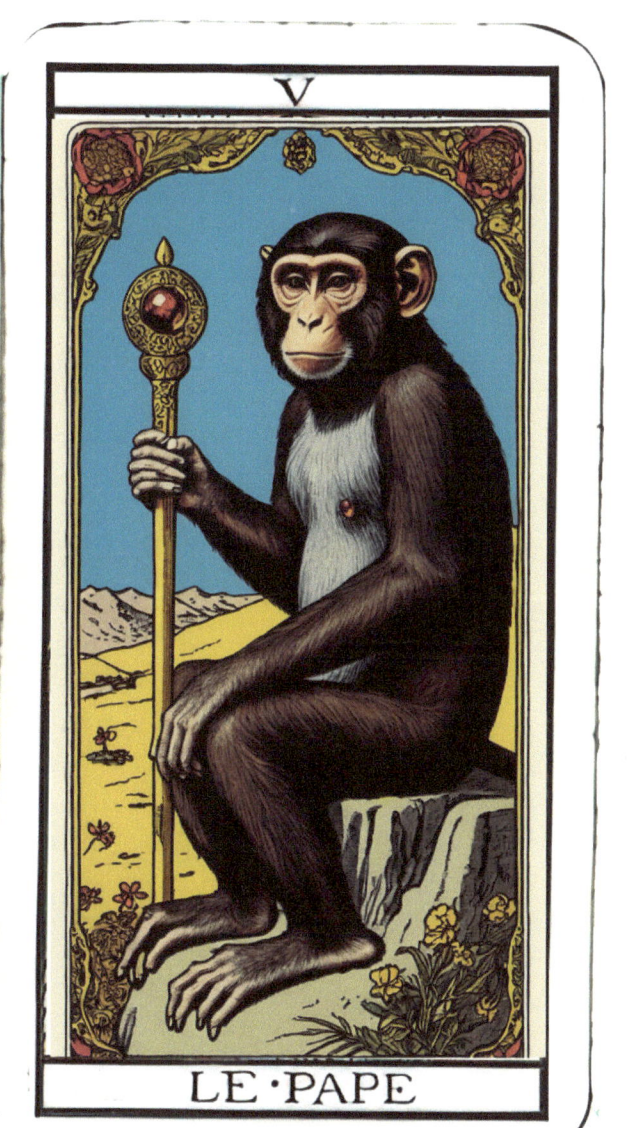

VI

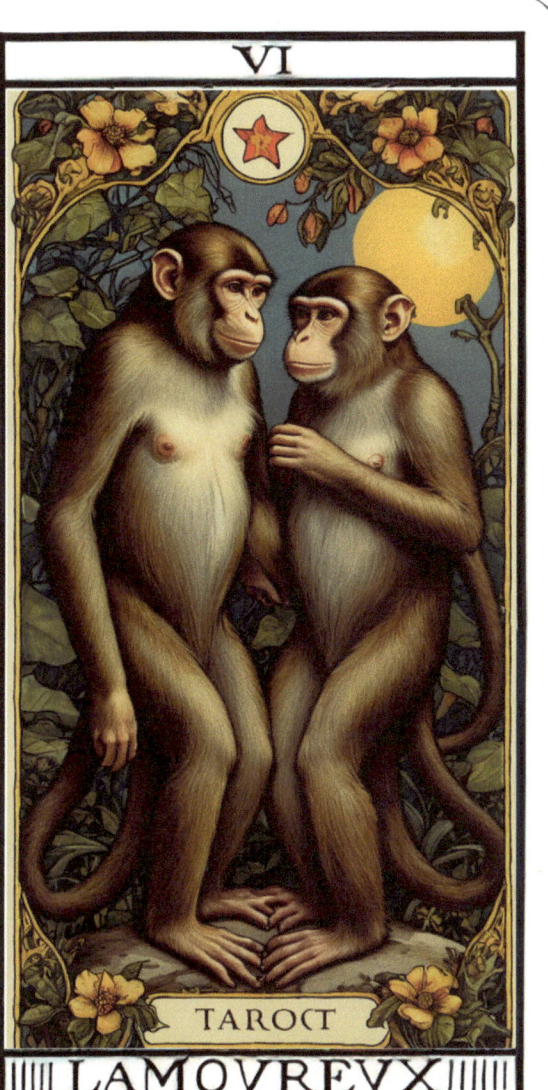

TAROCT

LAMOVREVX

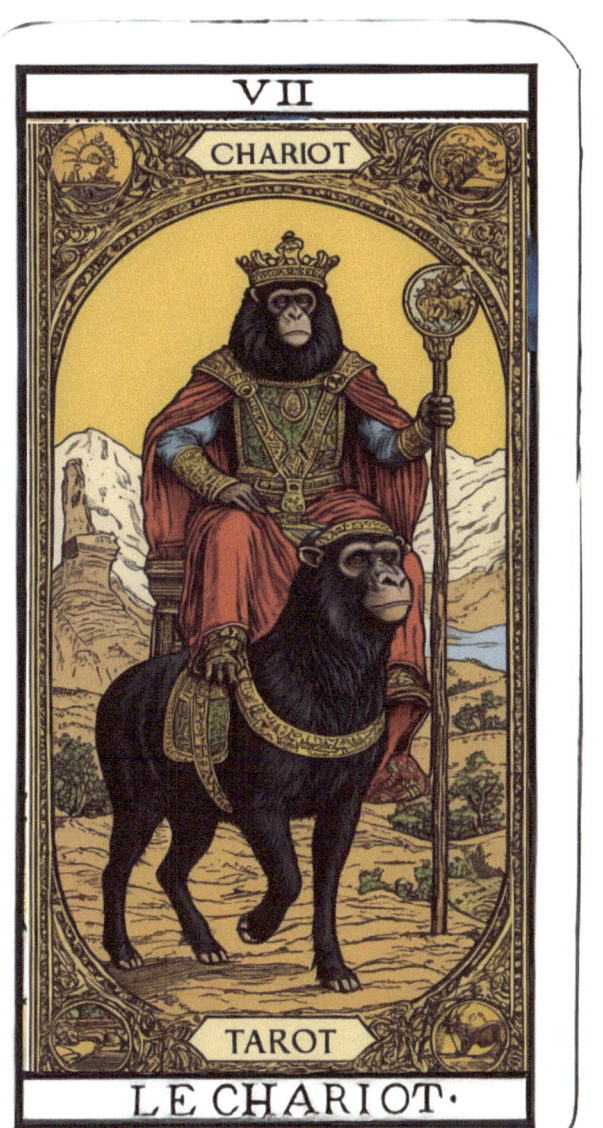

VII

CHARIOT

TAROT

LE CHARIOT·

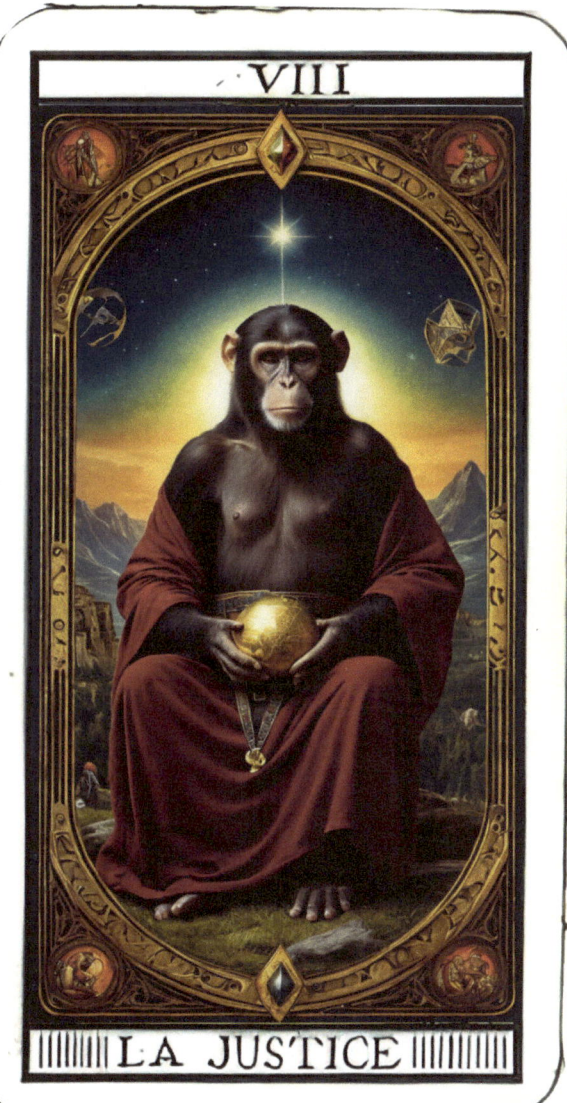

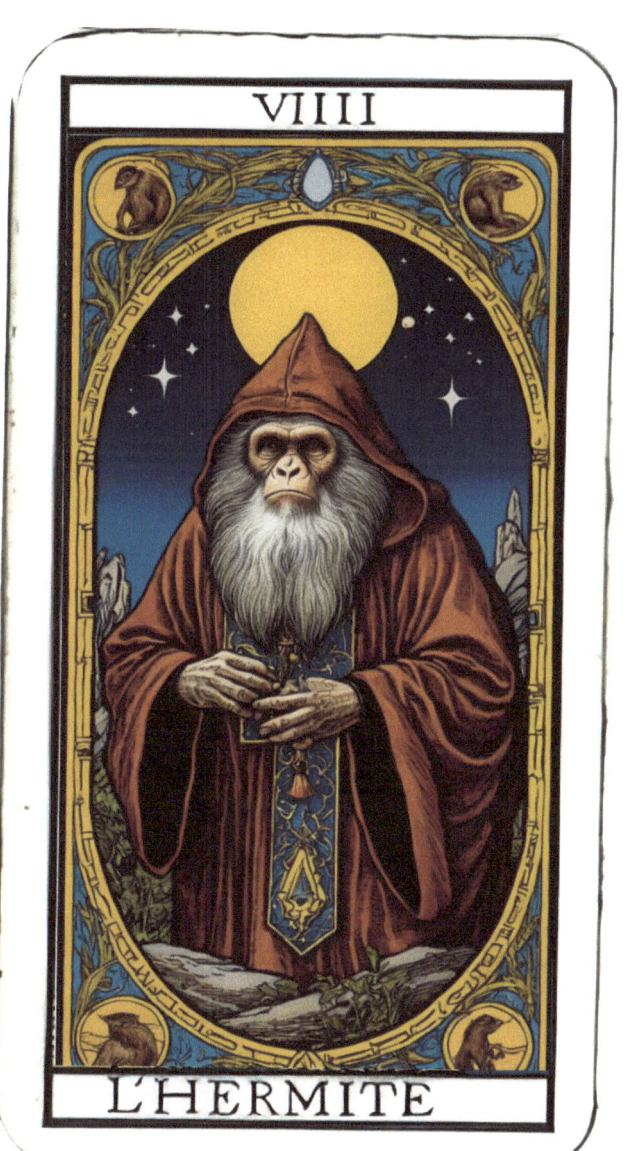

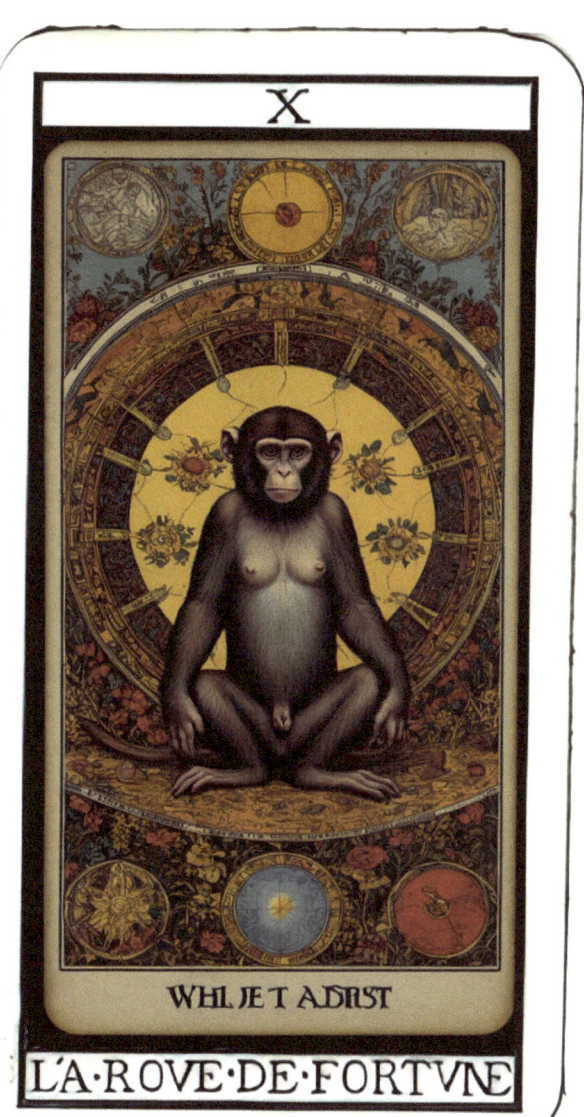

X

WHL JE T ADRST

L'A·ROVE·DE·FORTVNE

XI

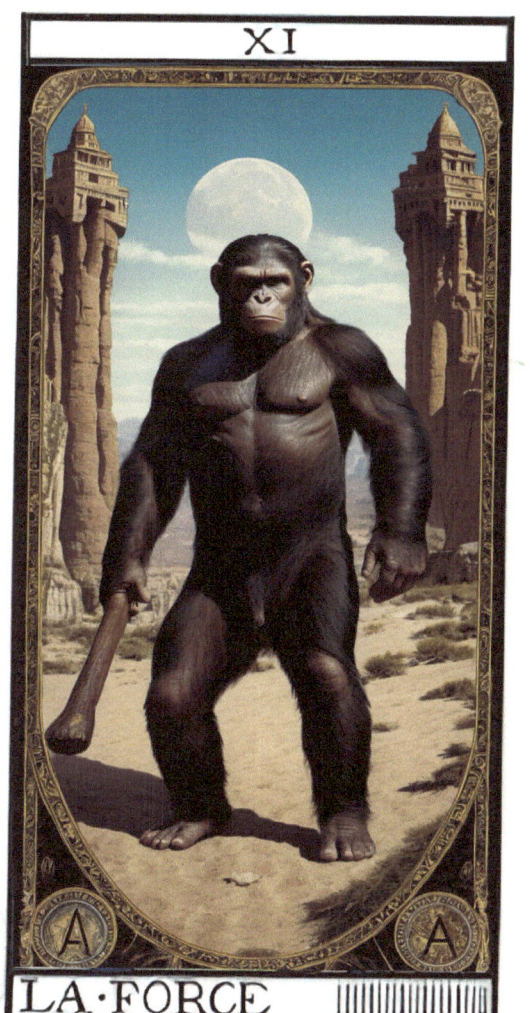

LA·FORCE

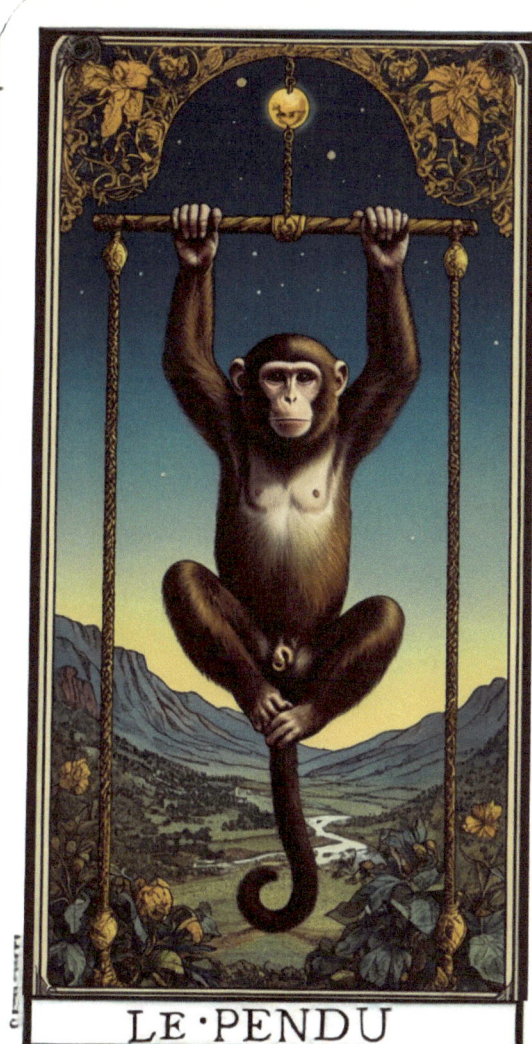

LE · PENDU

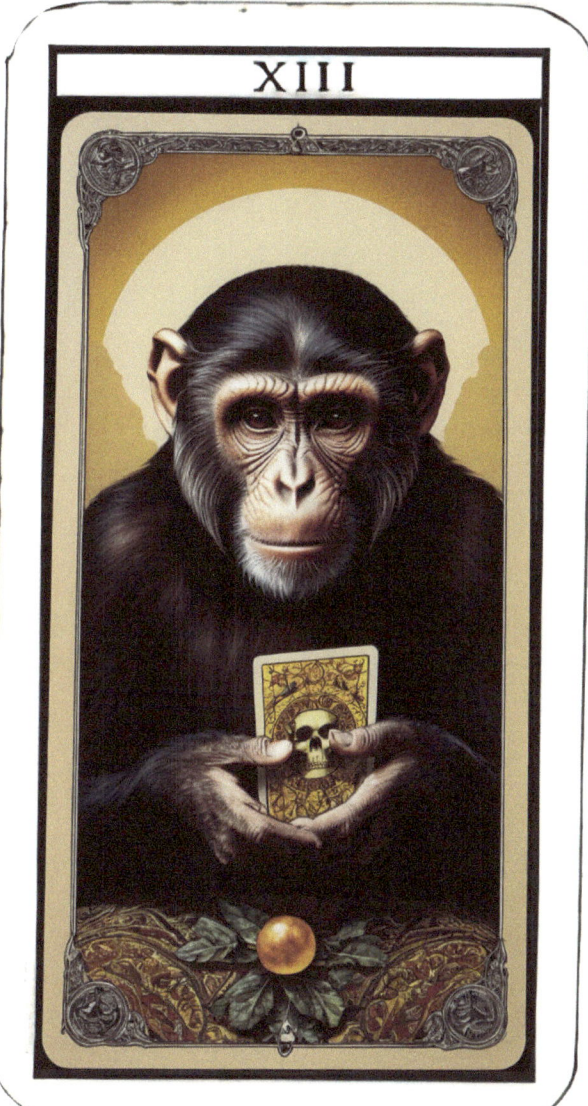

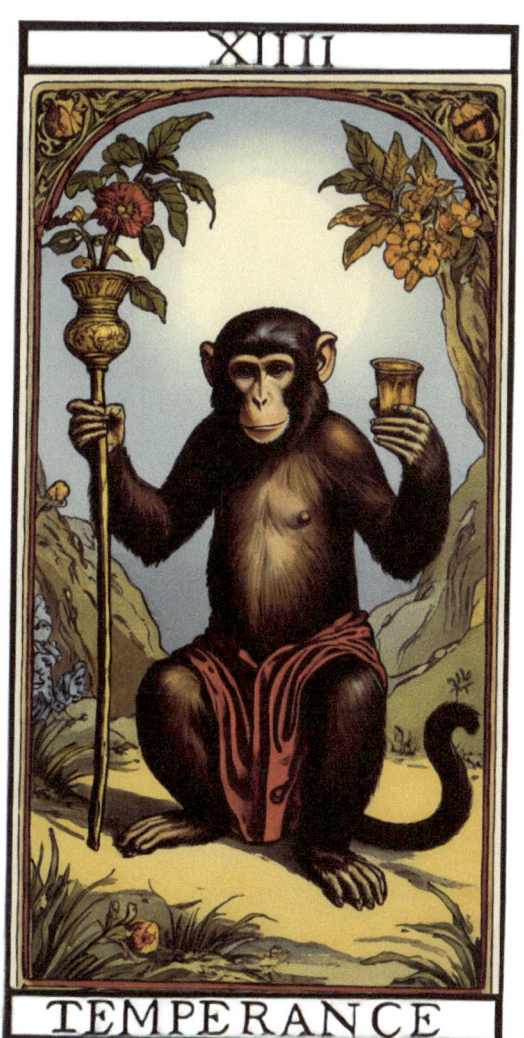

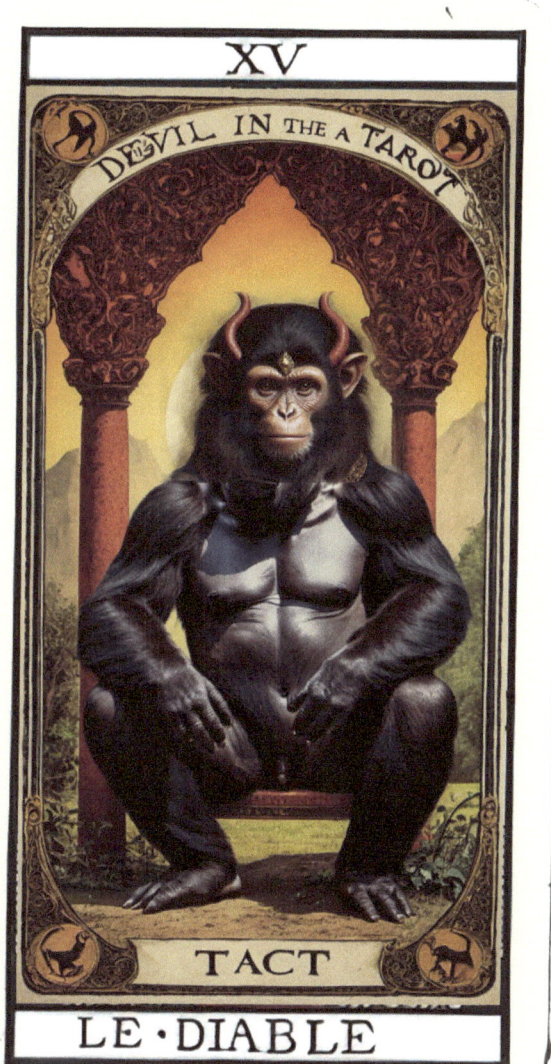

XV

DEVIL IN THE A TAROT

TACT

LE · DIABLE

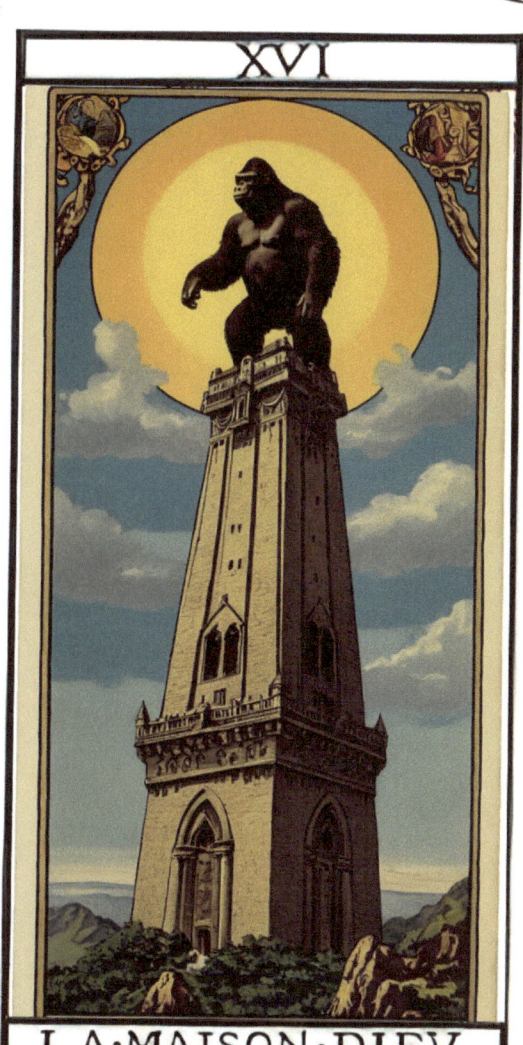

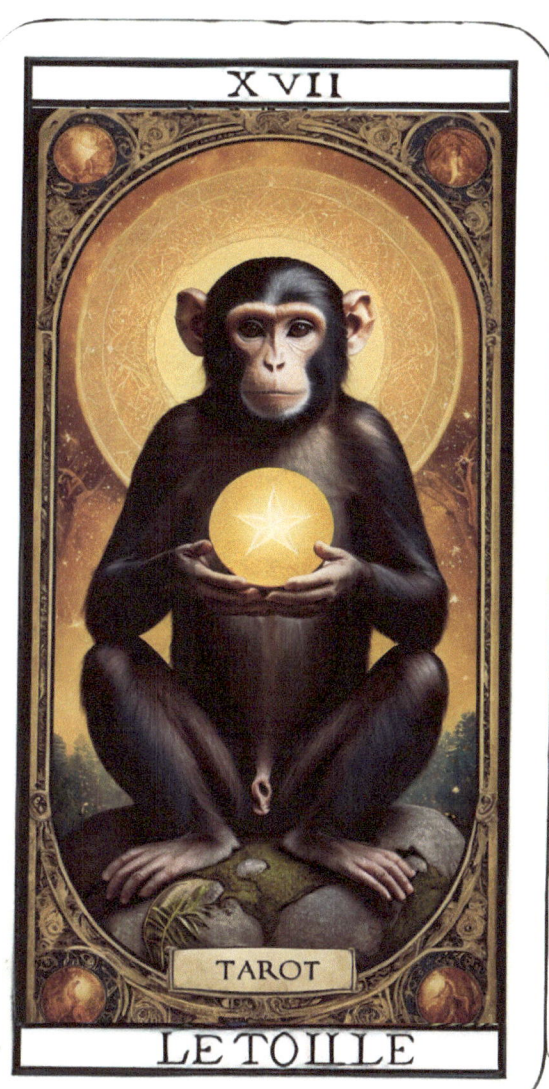

XVII

TAROT

LE TOILLE

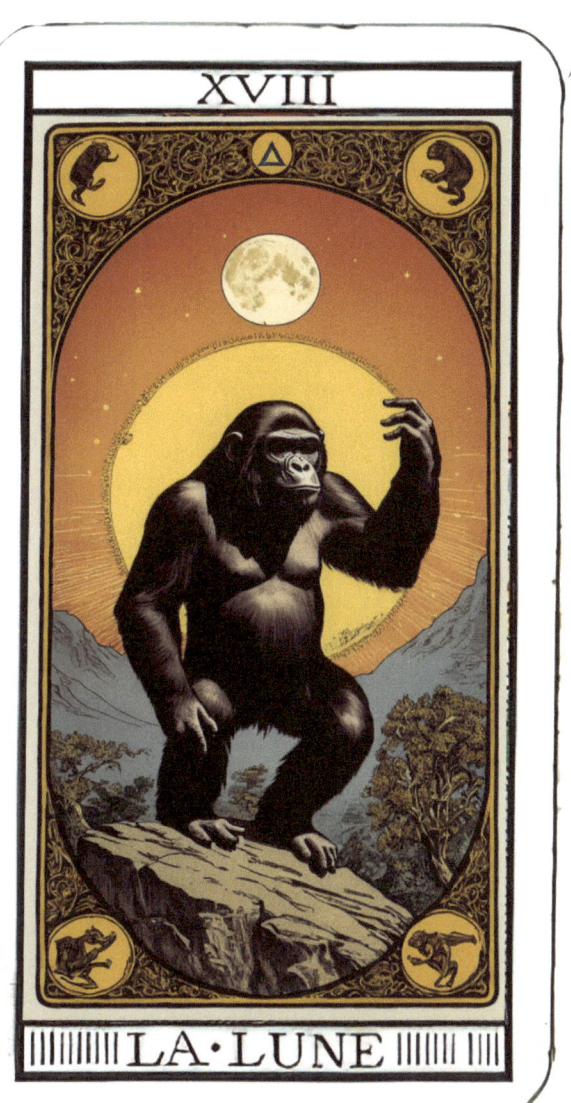

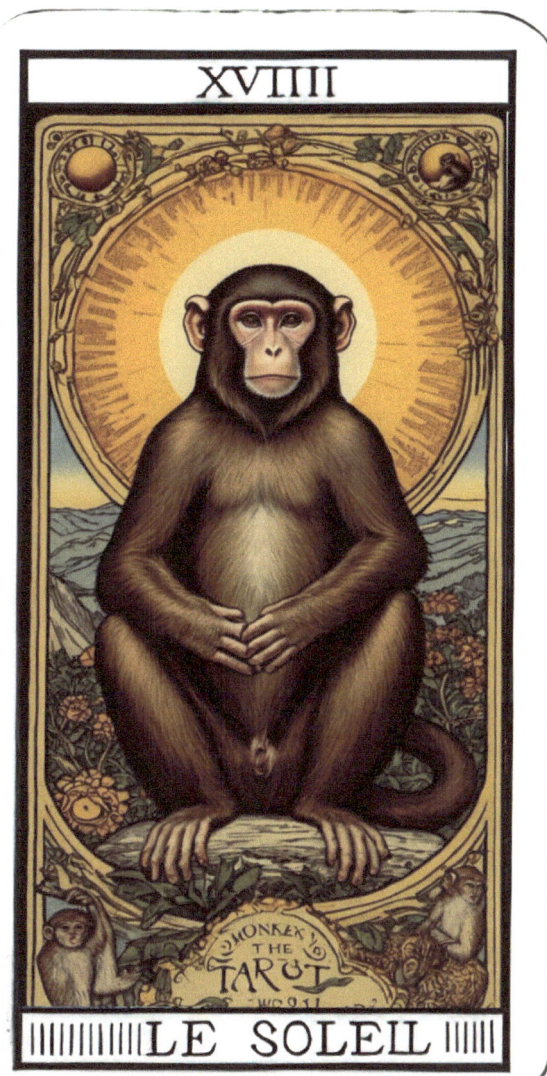

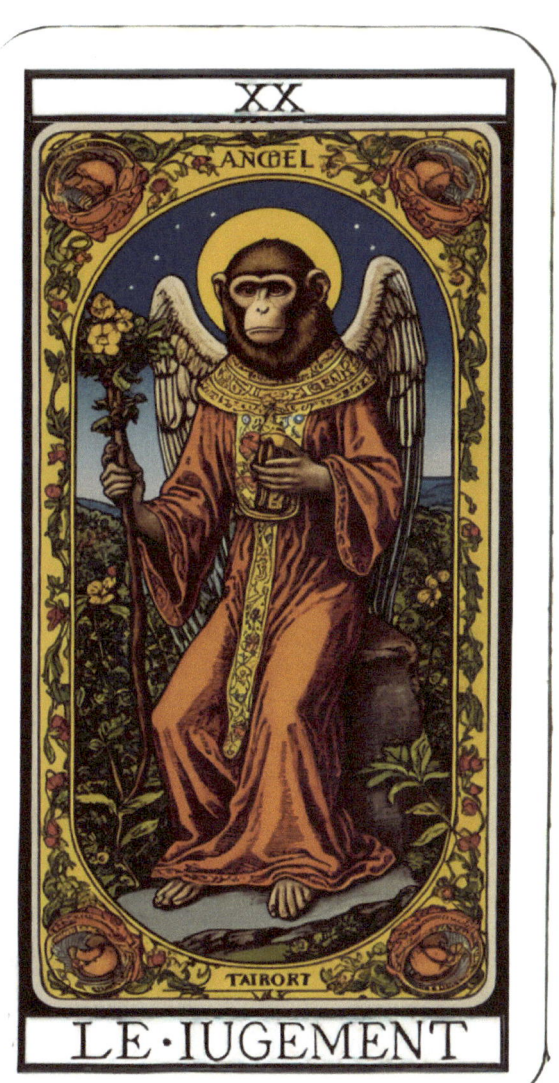

XX

ANGEL

TAIRORT

LE·IUGEMENT

XXI

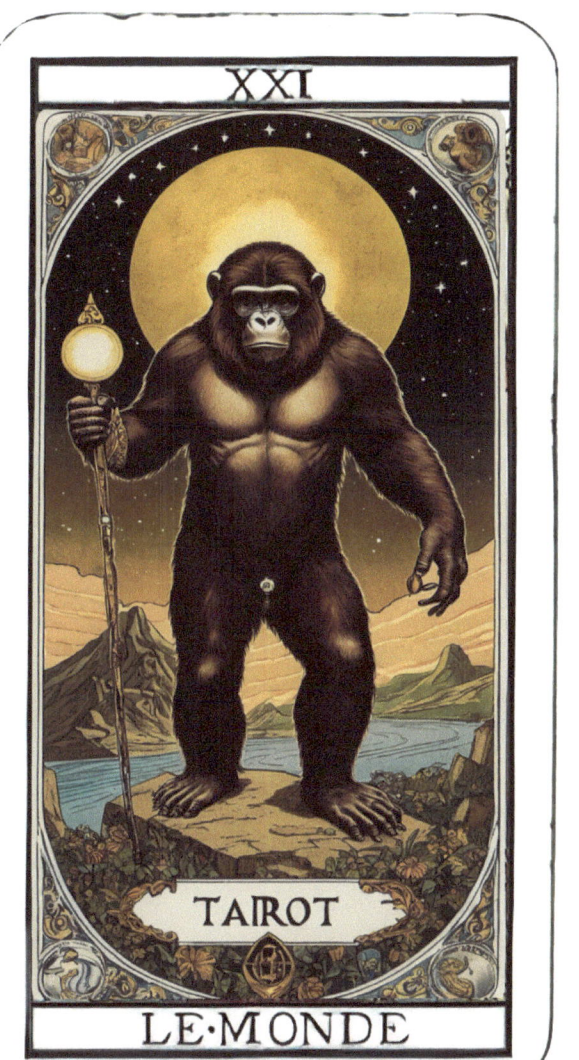

TAIROT

LE·MONDE

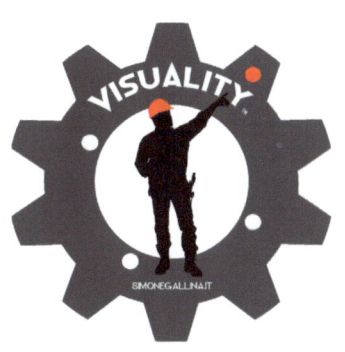

VISUALITYtarots

www.simonegallina.it

© 2063